KHANH PHAN

The Architecture of Being Human

Volume 2 The Emotional System: Foundations

First published by Khanh Phan 2025

Copyright © 2025 by Khanh Phan

All rights reserved. No part of this publication may be reproduced, stored or transmitted in any form or by any means, electronic, mechanical, photocopying, recording, scanning, or otherwise without written permission from the publisher. It is illegal to copy this book, post it to a website, or distribute it by any other means without permission.

This book reflects personal experience and perspective. It is not intended as medical, psychological, or legal advice.

This volume continues from The Architecture of Being Human, Volume 1. It assumes familiarity with the structural framework established there.

First edition

ISBN (print): 978-1-971116-04-4
ISBN (digital): 978-1-971116-03-7

PROLOGUE — What Emotion Is (Before It Becomes a Problem)

Emotion is often encountered only after it has become difficult.

By the time most people pay attention to what they feel, something has already gone wrong. The body is tense. The mind is explaining. The system is trying to regain control. Emotion appears as a disruption — something to manage, suppress, understand, or get past.

But this is not where emotion begins.

Emotion begins long before interpretation.
Before narrative.
Before judgment.

It begins as information.

Not information about the world in the abstract, but information about *fit* — about whether what is happening can be integrated without destabilizing the system.

This volume does not approach emotion as an experience to be improved or a state to be regulated. It approaches emotion as a system — one that already knows what it is doing, even when it overwhelms.

Overwhelm is not evidence of failure.
Confusion is not evidence of immaturity.
Intensity is not evidence of dysfunction.

They are signs that emotion has been misunderstood.

Most frameworks try to intervene at the point where emotion has already escalated. They offer strategies for calming, reframing, or controlling what is felt. This book steps earlier.

It stays with emotion before it becomes personal.
Before it becomes a story.
Before it becomes something you believe is *you*.

Nothing here asks you to change what you feel.
Nothing asks you to resolve it.
Nothing asks you to behave differently.

It asks only that emotion be seen accurately — as a system operating to preserve coherence.

When emotion is understood at this level, something subtle happens.
It stops feeling like an enemy.
And it stops demanding immediate action.

PART I — WHAT EMOTION IS

Emotion is rarely encountered at its origin.

Most people meet emotion only after it has already taken shape — as reaction, feeling, or problem. By then, explanation is already active, meaning has begun to form, and the system is responding rather than registering.

This part stays earlier.

Before emotion feels personal.
Before it becomes something to manage, regulate, or resolve.
Before it is treated as evidence of weakness, truth, or failure.

Here, emotion is approached as a functional movement within the system — not as expression, not as narrative, not as identity. It is examined at the point where it first appears, before it hardens into reaction or explanation.

Nothing in this part asks the reader to change what they feel.
Nothing asks for control or correction.

It establishes sequence.

When the origin of emotion is placed correctly, much of what feels confusing about emotional experience loses urgency. Not because emotion disappears, but because it is no longer mistaken for something it is not.

This part restores that placement.

CHAPTER 1 — Emotion Is Not a Reaction

Emotion is often described as something that happens *in response* to events.

Someone says something.
Something goes wrong.
A memory is triggered.
Emotion appears.

This framing makes emotion feel secondary — an effect caused by the world. It also makes emotion feel unreliable, because reactions can appear exaggerated, misplaced, or disproportionate.

But emotion does not arise *after* events.
It arises during explanation.

Before the mind decides what something means, the system has already registered whether what is happening can be integrated without destabilizing what it is already holding together.

This registration is not deliberate.
It is not chosen.
It is not learned consciously —
it reflects what the system learned had to be noticed quickly.

It is orientation.

Emotion is the system adjusting its position in relation to what is present — long before a conclusion is reached.

This is why emotion often arrives without permission.
Why it can contradict your understanding.
Why it can persist even after insight.

Emotion is not reacting to meaning.
Meaning is responding to emotion.

Once this order is seen, emotional responses stop feeling arbitrary. They become legible as signals — not instructions, not judgments, not truths — but indicators of where the system is being asked to stretch beyond what it can currently hold.

CHAPTER 2 — Emotion Is Not Thought

Because emotion often appears alongside explanation, it is easy to confuse the two.

A sensation arises.
A meaning follows.
The explanation feels inseparable from what is felt.

This makes it seem as though emotion is produced by thinking — as though changing the explanation should change the feeling. When it does not, emotion is treated as irrational, stubborn, or unresolved.

But emotion does not originate in thought.
Thought arrives after the system has already shifted.

Before language forms, before reasons are assembled, the body has already registered whether what is happening can be held without strain. That registration is what emotion carries forward.

This is why emotion can contradict understanding.

You may know why something happened and still feel tension.
You may agree with a decision and still feel unsettled.
You may understand someone's behavior and still feel distance or irritation.

If emotion were created by explanation, understanding would resolve it. But understanding often changes nothing.

This is not because emotion resists logic.
It is because emotion is not operating at the level of logic.

The mind translates what the system is already responding to. It names, contextualizes, and evaluates the signal. This translation happens quickly and automatically, shaped by memory, association, and learned pattern.

When this translation is mistaken for the source of emotion, effort is misdirected.

People try to think differently.
Reframe.
Convince themselves.

Sometimes this reduces intensity.
Rarely does it complete what the signal is doing.

Emotion is not asking for better explanation.
It is asking to be recognized where the system first learned to register danger quickly.

Once the sequence is seen clearly — registration first, explanation second — emotion stops being treated as something that must be reasoned away.

It becomes understandable.

CHAPTER 3 — Emotion Is Not Identity

Because emotion arrives early and repeats often, it is easy for it to become personal.

A reaction appears again and again.
A familiar tension returns.
The same emotional pressure shows up across different situations.

Over time, the repetition invites a conclusion.

This is just how I am.
I'm an anxious person.
I'm sensitive.
I'm easily irritated.

Emotion becomes identity.

This does not happen because the emotion is expressive or meaningful.
It happens because the system learned something once and kept using it.

When the system learns to identify danger quickly, it prioritizes speed over precision. The signal that preserved stability is reused whenever a situation resembles what was learned before — even loosely.

The repetition is not reflection.

It is efficiency.

This is why triggers form.

A trigger is not a cause.
It is a resemblance.

When a present situation carries features that resemble what was learned before, the system reuses the same signal. It does not check whether the situation is identical. It checks whether it is close enough to warrant the same response.

Because the signal appears automatically and without conscious choice, it feels like part of you. The emotion seems to come *from you*, rather than *through you*.

This is where identification forms.

Not as belief.
As familiarity.

The system recognizes its own signal and treats it as a trait. The faster the signal appears, the more convincing it feels. What was once a protective response becomes interpreted as personality.

This is why identity-based explanations feel convincing but incomplete.

Saying *"this is just who I am"* does not resolve the emotion.
Saying *"this is my personality"* does not reduce its intensity.

Because identity is not where the signal originates.

Resolution does not require removing triggers from the world.

CHAPTER 3 — EMOTION IS NOT IDENTITY

It requires removing the system's need to respond to them.

When the emotion that once enforced protection completes, the relationship to the trigger changes. The situation may still be noticed, but it no longer activates the same signal.

What disappears is not awareness.
It is urgency —
the impulse to defend,
to explain,
to justify.

Identification amplifies emotion by collapsing distance. When emotion is treated as identity, there is no separation between signal and self. The signal is no longer something occurring — it becomes something *being*.

This is why emotion feels heavier when it is personalized.
Why shame, self-judgment, and resignation often follow.
Why effort increases but resolution does not.

Observation changes this relationship, but it does not change origin.

Seeing emotion as not-you creates space.
It reduces reactivity.
It interrupts escalation.

But disidentification alone does not end the signal.

Because the system is not defending identity.
It is defending stability.

Emotion stops being treated as identity when its function is placed correctly — as a learned response that once preserved coherence, not as a defining feature of the self.

When this distinction becomes clear, something subtle shifts.

The emotion can still appear.
The signal can still register.

But it no longer defines.

From here, the emotional system becomes legible enough to be mapped —
not by label or intensity, but by structure.

That is where the next part begins.

PART II — THE EMOTIONAL ARCHITECTURE

Emotion does not operate as a single event.

It moves through a system.

By the time emotion is felt clearly, several things have already happened. The body has registered change. The mind has begun translating. Attention has shifted. What feels like one experience is actually a sequence.

This part makes that sequence visible.

Not to analyze it.
Not to intervene.
To place it correctly.

Here, emotion is examined by **where it appears**, not by what it is called or how intense it feels. This allows different emotional experiences to be understood without ranking them, managing them, or turning them into problems.

Some emotional signals arise quickly and pass once direction is corrected.
Others remain longer, regulating behavior and internal balance.
Others appear only after something has already shifted, as states rather than

reactions.

These differences are not about strength.
They are about location.

Without this map, emotions are often misread. Surface reactions are treated as deep truths. Deeper signals are treated as personal flaws. Effort is applied at the wrong point, and confusion follows.

This part does not teach how to change emotion.
It shows where emotion is already moving.

By placing emotion within the body–mind system clearly, what once felt chaotic begins to feel organized. Not resolved. Not reduced.

Just placed.

From here, the emotional system becomes visible enough to be followed — layer by layer — without forcing it to do anything it is not ready to do.

CHAPTER 4 — The Body as the Origin

Emotion begins in the body.

Not as feeling.
Not as story.
As physical registration.

Before emotion is named or recognized, the body has already detected change. Muscles adjust. Breath shifts. Energy gathers or withdraws. These changes often happen below the threshold of attention.

A tightness in the chest.
A heaviness in the stomach.
A readiness in the arms or jaw.

By the time emotion is felt clearly, these changes have already occurred.

This is why emotion can feel sudden.
The body moves first.

The body does not assess meaning.
It does not analyze intention.
It does not consider explanation.

It registers whether what is happening can be held without strain.

When something exceeds what the system learned it could safely manage, the body responds immediately. This response is not emotional in itself. It is preparatory. It adjusts posture, breathing, and readiness in anticipation of what may be required.

This is the earliest point of emotion.

Because this registration happens quickly and without language, it is easy to overlook. People often become aware of emotion only once the mind has translated these bodily changes into feeling and explanation.

But the body has already moved.

This is why emotional responses can feel disconnected from conscious understanding. The body is not reacting to meaning. It is responding to load.

What the body learned to watch for matters here.

At some point, certain conditions required rapid adjustment to preserve stability. The body learned what to tense for, what to brace against, and what to prepare to avoid. These adjustments were useful then, so they were kept.

When present conditions resemble those earlier demands, the same bodily response is reused. The body does not check whether the situation is identical. It checks whether it is close enough to require the same readiness.

This is not memory in the usual sense.
It is learned readiness.

Because this response is physical, it feels immediate and real. The body is already preparing before the mind has decided what is happening. By the time emotion becomes conscious, the body has already taken a position.

CHAPTER 4 — THE BODY AS THE ORIGIN

This is why emotion cannot be resolved by thought alone.
The body has already responded.

Understanding this changes how emotion is approached. Instead of asking why you feel a certain way, attention can move to where the response began — not to control it, but to recognize it accurately.

The body is not expressing emotion.
It is initiating it.

From here, the role of the mind becomes clearer.

CHAPTER 5 — The Mind as Translator

After the body registers change, the mind responds.

It does not initiate emotion.
It translates it.

The mind takes what the body has already detected and begins to organize it into something understandable. Sensation becomes feeling. Feeling becomes explanation. Explanation becomes meaning.

This translation happens quickly. Often automatically. By the time you notice what you feel, the mind has already been at work.

A tightness becomes irritation.
A heaviness becomes sadness.
A surge of energy becomes anger or urgency.

These labels do not create the emotion.
They give it form.

The mind's role is not to decide whether emotion is valid. It tries to make sense of what the body has already signaled. It asks implicit questions:

What is this?
What does it relate to?

CHAPTER 5 — THE MIND AS TRANSLATOR

What should I do with it?

To answer, the mind draws from memory, pattern, and past experience. It compares what is happening now to what has happened before. This is how context forms.

Because this process relies on what was learned earlier, the translation is not always precise. The mind works with resemblance, not certainty. It looks for what fits closely enough to explain the signal.

This is where emotional distortion can begin.

A present sensation may be translated through an old reference.
A current situation may be explained using a past outcome.

The translation feels convincing because it arrives alongside the sensation. But explanation is not the same as accuracy.

When the mind's translation is mistaken for the source of emotion, confusion follows. People try to correct the explanation, assuming that changing the story will change the feeling.

Sometimes it does.
Often it does not.

This is because the mind is working downstream. It can shape experience, soften intensity, or escalate it — but it did not initiate the signal.

The mind is not creating emotion.
It is responding to it.

This is why different explanations can accompany the same bodily response. The sensation remains while the story changes. This is also why insight can coexist with emotional pressure. The explanation updates, but the body has not yet released.

The mind is useful here. It brings clarity, sequence, and meaning. But when it is asked to resolve what it did not start, it becomes overworked.

Understanding the mind as translator restores its proper role. It no longer has to justify, override, or eliminate emotion. It simply reflects what the system is already responding to.

With this distinction in place, the final part of the architecture becomes visible — the role of observation.

CHAPTER 6 — The Observer as Stabilizer

Observation enters after sensation and translation.

It does not interrupt the process.
It changes the relationship to it.

When emotion is observed, distance appears. The signal is no longer identical with the self. Reaction slows. Escalation softens. What once felt overwhelming becomes trackable.

This does not happen because emotion stops.
It happens because identification loosens.

The observer does not analyze emotion.
It notices it.

This noticing does not resolve the signal. It stabilizes the system by removing collapse. The emotion can exist without requiring immediate action or explanation.

This is why observation often brings relief but not completion.

The signal remains.
The pressure may still be present.

What changes is urgency.

The observer creates space.
It does not change origin.

This distinction matters.

Many people assume that because observation reduces intensity, it should also end emotion. When it does not, they believe something is wrong or incomplete.

Nothing is wrong.

Observation allows emotion to be present without taking over. It prevents escalation. It keeps the system from reacting to its own signal.

But the system is not finished yet.

The observer stabilizes experience by holding awareness steady while the body and mind continue their roles. It prevents confusion, not completion.

This is why observation alone cannot resolve emotion.
It was never meant to.

Its role is to make the process survivable and visible.

With the body initiating, the mind translating, and the observer stabilizing, the emotional architecture becomes clear.

What remains is not another layer — but variation within this structure.

Not all emotions move the same way.
Not all signals resolve at the same point.

CHAPTER 6 — THE OBSERVER AS STABILIZER

That is where the next part begins.

PART III — EMOTIONAL FAMILIES

Emotions do not all move the same way.

Some appear quickly and pass once direction is corrected.
Others remain, shaping behavior and internal balance.
Others appear only after something has already settled, as states rather than reactions.

These differences are often misunderstood as problems of intensity or control. An emotion that lingers is treated as excessive. An emotion that fades quickly is treated as insignificant.

But persistence is not a flaw.
It is a clue.

This part organizes emotions by **what they are doing**, not by what they are called. Each emotional family serves a different role in preserving stability. Each operates at a different depth within the system.

When emotions are grouped this way, confusion softens. What once felt random becomes ordered. Emotional experience stops being judged by how disruptive it is and starts being understood by what it is protecting.

This part does not name emotions to catalog them.
It places them by function.

CHAPTER 7 — Activating Emotions

Some emotions arise to mobilize the system.

They appear quickly.
They sharpen focus.
They prepare the body to act.

Anger, fear, urgency, and alarm belong to this family — not as problems, but as signals that something requires immediate adjustment.

These emotions activate when the system detects a threat to stability that cannot be ignored. Boundaries feel crossed. Safety feels uncertain. Direction needs correction.

The response is fast because delay would have carried risk when these signals were first learned.

Activating emotions do not ask for reflection.
They ask for readiness.

This is why they often feel intense. Intensity here is not excess. It is efficiency. The system is gathering energy to respond.

When the adjustment is made — when a boundary becomes clear or direction is restored — these emotions often release quickly. They were never meant to linger.

When they do linger, it is not because they are out of control. It is because something essential has not yet settled.

Activating emotions are not asking to be suppressed.
They are asking whether action is still required.

CHAPTER 8 — Withdrawing Emotions

Other emotions move in the opposite direction.

Instead of mobilizing the system, they slow it down.
Energy pulls inward.
Attention narrows.

Sadness, heaviness, fatigue, and grief belong to this family.

These emotions appear when something the system relied on is no longer available. A role, a relationship, a future, or a sense of direction has changed. The system cannot move forward as it did before.

Withdrawing emotions create space.

They reduce outward engagement so the system can reorganize internally. This slowing is not collapse. It is recalibration.

These emotions often feel heavy because they are not responding to a moment. They are responding to loss or change at a structural level.

Because reorganization takes time, withdrawing emotions do not resolve quickly. Trying to push past them often increases strain. The system resists being rushed while it is rebuilding.

Withdrawing emotions are not asking for motivation.
They are asking for space to reorganize.

CHAPTER 9 — Social-Regulatory Emotions

Some emotions exist to regulate alignment within a social context.

Guilt, shame, embarrassment, and self-consciousness belong to this family.

These emotions arise when behavior, impulse, or expression moves out of alignment with what the system learned was required to remain accepted, included, or safe with others.

They do not regulate action directly.
They regulate *fit*.

Guilt signals misalignment with an internal standard.
Shame signals perceived risk to belonging.

These emotions often feel personal because they turn inward. The system monitors itself to prevent outcomes that once carried consequence.

Social-regulatory emotions are learned early and reinforced often. They tend to persist because social stability was rarely optional.

These emotions are not evidence of moral failure.
They are evidence of learned consequence.

They resolve not through self-criticism or reassurance, but through understanding what standard is being enforced and whether it is still required.

CHAPTER 10 — Why Persistence Differs

When emotions are grouped by family, persistence becomes understandable.

An activating emotion may resolve once action is no longer required.
A withdrawing emotion may remain until reorganization is complete.
A social-regulatory emotion may persist as long as a standard remains unquestioned.

Persistence does not mean something is wrong.
It means the function is not finished.

Trying to resolve all emotions the same way creates frustration. Speed-based signals are treated as deep problems. Deep signals are treated as reactions to override.

When the function is misread, effort is applied at the wrong level.

Understanding which family an emotion belongs to does not resolve it.
It prevents misinterpretation.

The system is no longer asked to do something it is not ready to do.

CHAPTER 11 — When Emotions Overlap

More than one emotional family can be active at once.

You may feel anger and guilt together.
Sadness and relief.
Fear and excitement.

This is not contradiction.
It is layered signaling.

Different parts of the system can be responding to different demands at the same time. One emotion may be mobilizing action. Another may be enforcing alignment. Another may be reorganizing meaning.

When these layers are not distinguished, emotional experience feels confusing or overwhelming. The system appears to be working against itself.

In reality, it is responding to more than one requirement at once.

Clarity does not come from eliminating layers.
It comes from recognizing them.

PART IV — DISTORTION & OVERLOAD

Emotion does not become difficult because it exists.
It becomes difficult when it is misread.

Once emotion is mistaken for reaction, thought, or identity, the system begins responding to the signal instead of allowing it to do its work. This is where distortion, suppression, and overload enter.

This part does not frame these responses as mistakes.
They are adaptations.

They arise when the system is trying to remain stable without a clear map of what emotion is doing.

CHAPTER 12 — Emotional Distortion

Emotional distortion occurs when a signal is interpreted at the wrong level.

A surface reaction is treated as a deep truth.
A deep signal is treated as a personal flaw.
A temporary state is treated as permanent meaning.

This misplacement changes how emotion is experienced.

A brief activating emotion may be translated as danger everywhere.
A withdrawing emotion may be interpreted as failure or weakness.
A social-regulatory emotion may be taken as evidence of who you are.

The emotion itself has not changed.
Its placement has.

Distortion does not come from exaggeration.
It comes from compression.

Complex signals are reduced into single explanations. The system tries to simplify what feels confusing so it can respond quickly. This worked when speed mattered more than accuracy.

Once this compression happens, emotion feels heavier than it is. The signal is carrying more meaning than it was designed to hold.

CHAPTER 12 — EMOTIONAL DISTORTION

Distortion is not lying.
It is overloading.

When emotion is placed correctly — by function and location — distortion softens on its own. Nothing needs to be corrected.

CHAPTER 13 — Suppression, Avoidance, and Shutdown

When emotion feels overwhelming or unsafe, the system looks for ways to reduce exposure.

Suppression, avoidance, and shutdown are not strategies chosen consciously. They are responses that appear when expression or awareness once increased risk.

Suppression limits expression.
Avoidance limits contact.
Shutdown limits sensation.

Each serves the same purpose: reducing load.

These responses are often learned early. When showing emotion led to consequence — rejection, ridicule, escalation, or loss of safety — the system adapted.

These adaptations persist not because they are effective now, but because they once were.

Suppression does not erase emotion.
It delays it.

CHAPTER 13 — SUPPRESSION, AVOIDANCE, AND SHUTDOWN

Avoidance does not remove emotion.
It reroutes it.

Shutdown does not end emotion.
It reduces capacity to feel it.

None of these responses are failures. They are evidence of protection operating without updated information.

When emotion is misunderstood, these adaptations often intensify. The system works harder to keep itself intact.

CHAPTER 14 — Emotional Backlog

Emotion that is delayed does not disappear.

When signals cannot complete — because expression felt unsafe, awareness felt overwhelming, or capacity was exceeded — they remain active beneath the surface.

This accumulation is often referred to as emotional backlog.

Backlog does not mean emotion was ignored.
It means it was deferred.

Over time, deferred signals stack. The system carries more than it was designed to hold at once. This is when emotional experience begins to feel disproportionate.

A small event triggers a large response.
Fatigue appears without a clear cause.
Irritation surfaces unexpectedly.

These responses are not about the present moment alone. They are about accumulated load.

Backlog is not resolved by release alone.
It resolves when signals are allowed to complete at the level they originated.

CHAPTER 14 — EMOTIONAL BACKLOG

Until then, the system compensates by narrowing tolerance and reducing capacity.

CHAPTER 15 — Emotional Capacity

Emotional capacity is not about strength or resilience.
It is about load.

Every system has a limit to how much it can hold at once without destabilizing. When capacity is exceeded, emotion becomes overwhelming — not because it is too intense, but because there is too much active at once.

Capacity is influenced by:

- accumulated backlog
- ongoing stress
- lack of recovery
- repeated activation without completion

When capacity is low, even mild signals feel disruptive. This often leads to self-judgment or attempts to control emotion more tightly.

But control does not increase capacity.
Restoration does.

This volume does not address how capacity is rebuilt. That belongs later.

Here, it is enough to recognize that overwhelm is often a volume problem,

CHAPTER 15 — EMOTIONAL CAPACITY

not a content problem.

CHAPTER 16 — Emotional Honesty

Emotional honesty is often mistaken for expression.

It is not saying everything you feel.
It is not acting on emotion.
It is not intensity.

Emotional honesty is the ability to recognize what is present without distortion.

It means allowing a signal to exist without explaining it away, personalizing it, or forcing it to change. It is accuracy, not disclosure.

When emotion is met honestly, it stops needing to escalate to be noticed.

This does not resolve emotion.
It allows resolution to become possible.

CLOSING PASSAGE — What Remains

Something may already feel different.

Not because emotions have stopped.
Not because anything has been resolved.
But because the pressure around them has eased.

You may notice that feelings arrive without the same urgency.
That reactions no longer demand immediate meaning.
That the familiar need to explain what you feel has softened.

This is not control.
It is not calm.
It is not mastery.

What has loosened is misplacement.

Emotion no longer needs to prove anything about you.
It no longer needs to justify itself.
It no longer has to be managed in order to be allowed.

The body can register without alarm.
The mind can translate without certainty.
Signals can move without becoming conclusions.

Nothing here requires you to feel differently.
Nothing requires you to feel better.

What changes is the strain of believing that what you feel must be fixed, named, or carried forward as meaning.

You may notice moments where emotion passes without leaving a mark.
Moments where a response rises and settles without explanation.
Moments where nothing needs to be decided.

This can feel subtle.
Almost anticlimactic.
As if something important has stepped back quietly rather than ending.

What has stepped back is confusion.

Emotion has been returned to its place — not as a problem to solve, but as movement that once made sense and no longer needs to be defended.

You don't need to hold anything here.

And when nothing needs to be held,
the system naturally begins to settle.

www.ingramcontent.com/pod-product-compliance
Lightning Source LLC
Chambersburg PA
CBHW032104040426
42449CB00007B/1185